Cambridge **Discovery Education**™
▶ **INTERACTIVE READERS**

Series editor: Bob Hastings

BOUNCE!
THE WONDERFUL WORLD OF RUBBER

Karmel Schreyer

CAMBRIDGE UNIVERSITY PRESS
Cambridge, New York, Melbourne, Madrid, Cape Town,
Singapore, São Paulo, Delhi, Mexico City

Cambridge University Press
32 Avenue of the Americas, New York, NY 10013-2473, USA

www.cambridge.org
Information on this title: www.cambridge.org/9781107641549

© Cambridge University Press 2014

This publication is in copyright. Subject to statutory exception and to the provisions of relevant collective licensing agreements, no reproduction of any part may take place without the written permission of Cambridge University Press.

First published 2014

Printed in Hong Kong, China, by Golden Cup Printing Company Limited

A catalog record for this publication is available from the British Library.

Library of Congress Cataloging-in-Publication Data

Schreyer, Karmel.
  Bounce! the wonderful world of rubber / Karmel Schreyer.
     pages cm. -- (Cambridge discovery interactive readers)
  ISBN 978-1-107-64154-9 (pbk. : alk. paper)
  1. Rubber--Juvenile literature. 2. English language--Textbooks for foreign speakers. 3. Readers (Elementary) I. Title.

TS1890.S314 2014
678'.2--dc23

                          2013023896

ISBN 978-1-107-64154-9

Additional resources for this publication at www.cambridge.org

Cambridge University Press has no responsibility for the persistence or accuracy of URLs for external or third-party Internet Web sites referred to in this publication and does not guarantee that any content on such Web sites is, or will remain, accurate or appropriate.

Layout services, art direction, book design, and photo research: Q2ABillSMITH GROUP
Editorial services: Hyphen S.A.
Audio production: CityVox, New York
Video production: Q2ABillSMITH GROUP

Contents

Before You Read: Get Ready! 4

CHAPTER 1
Rubber, Rubber Everywhere! 6

CHAPTER 2
Tapping into Rubber's Special Qualities ... 8

CHAPTER 3
The Heart of Sports 12

CHAPTER 4
Rolling Along 18

CHAPTER 5
What Do You Think? 24

After You Read 26

Answer Key 28

Glossary

Before You Read:
Get Ready!

Rubber is everywhere! Many people considered it a miracle[1] material at first. It was a natural product, but we needed it so much we found a way to make it ourselves. Now some people think we have too much of it!

Words to Know

Look at the pictures. Then complete the sentences below with the correct words.

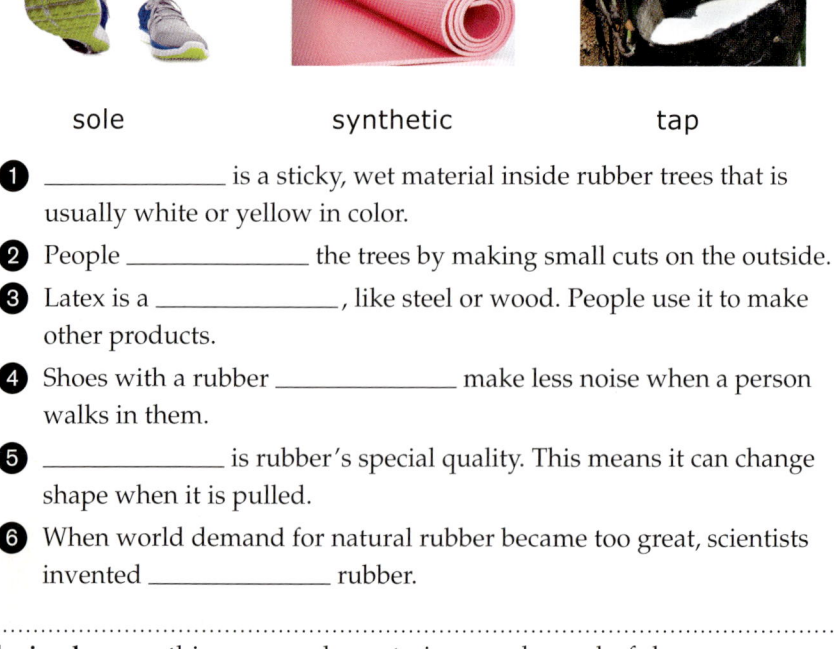

elasticity   latex   raw material

sole   synthetic   tap

❶ _____ is a sticky, wet material inside rubber trees that is usually white or yellow in color.

❷ People _____ the trees by making small cuts on the outside.

❸ Latex is a _____, like steel or wood. People use it to make other products.

❹ Shoes with a rubber _____ make less noise when a person walks in them.

❺ _____ is rubber's special quality. This means it can change shape when it is pulled.

❻ When world demand for natural rubber became too great, scientists invented _____ rubber.

....

[1] **miracle:** something unusual, mysterious, and wonderful

Words to Know

Look at the pictures of things made with rubber. Complete the chart below with the correct words.

artificial turf

asphalt

bungee cords

tire

treads

wetsuit

Recreation	Transport
1.	1.
2.	2.
3.	3.

APPLY

Can you think of any other common items that are made with rubber? Do you have anything right now that is made of rubber? Why is rubber useful for the item?

CHAPTER 1

Rubber, Rubber Everywhere!

LOOK AROUND YOU – HOW MANY THINGS CAN YOU SEE THAT ARE MADE WITH RUBBER? YOUR PENCIL ERASER, OF COURSE, BUT WHAT ABOUT YOUR BAG? YOUR SHOES? YOUR COMPUTER?

We use rubber in so many different ways, we hardly think about what an amazing material it is. It keeps us warm and dry, and it makes our lives easier, too. It is used to **manufacture** protective clothing, balloons, kitchen items, sportswear and equipment, tools, and so much more!

Rubber makes the games we play more fun and exciting. It gives balls – basketballs, tennis balls, even golf balls – their bounce. Rubber helps us get where we want to go, too, whether by bicycle, car, airplane, or on foot.

At first, rubber only came in its natural form, but rubber quickly became so important in our lives that we found a way to make it ourselves. Rubber has a long and interesting history. Europeans first learned of it when explorers came to the New World around 1500.

These Europeans were interested in the sticky **substance** the native people were using to light their homes, and to make their shoes, toys, and tools. It was brought back to Europe and, over time, other uses were found. When rubbed on paper, for example, it easily erases pencil marks – which is why the British still use the word "rubber" for "eraser"!

For almost 400 years, the Amazon region of Brazil was the world's main producer of rubber. Then, in 1876, British businessman Henry Wickham took 70,000 rubber-tree seeds from Brazil and secretly transported them to the Royal Botanic Gardens in London. Seedlings were grown, and then rubber **plantations** were set up in Africa and Asia. People began calling it "Indian rubber," and soon the whole world got used to its convenience. Can you imagine life without it?

Latex drips out of a rubber tree through shallow cuts in the bark.

CHAPTER 2

Tapping into Rubber's Special Qualities

RUBBER DOES NOT COME FROM NATURE IN THE FORM OF BOUNCY BALLS OR BIG BLACK TIRES.

Just as blood circulates in the bodies of people and animals, sap circulates in trees. Sap is a liquid that carries sugars and other nutrients [2] to feed different parts of a tree. The sap of rubber trees is called latex.

Latex is thick and sticky. It is found inside 10 percent of all flowering plants, including rubber plants. Latex is usually white, though some latex can be yellow, orange, or even red. There are many different species of rubber plants that produce latex, but the Pará rubber tree is the main species used for large-scale latex production.

[2] **nutrient:** any substance that plants and animals need to live and grow

Pará rubber trees first grew in South America, but as world demand for rubber increased, rubber plantations were developed in other parts of the world. Today, Thailand, Indonesia, and Malaysia are the world's top producers of rubber.

To obtain latex, you have to **tap** the rubber tree. A rubber tapper makes shallow cuts in the bark of a rubber tree. The liquid then begins to drip[3] out, and it is collected in buckets that hang on the trees.

The longer latex is in contact with the air, the thicker and stickier it becomes. Eventually the cut in the tree is covered by the latex and the dripping stops. So latex acts as a natural bandage.

A tree can be tapped every two or three days in the same general area before tappers have to move to a different place on the tree. It takes about seven years for a used section to heal[4] and become usable again.

[3]**drip:** fall in drops
[4]**heal:** become healthy again after an injury

Video Quest

Harvesting Latex

Watch this video to learn more about tapping rubber trees. Where in South America were rubber plantations first developed?

Each time a tree is tapped, it will produce about 30 grams of raw latex, adding up to about 11 kilograms a year. After the latex is collected, it is mixed with chemicals to help keep it thin and flowing. Later, acid[5] is added to make the mixture more solid. This mixture is then **rolled** into big, flat sheets to dry.

Drying can be done naturally by placing the sheets in the sun. The rubber sheets can also be dried by placing them in a smokehouse – rather like pizzas in an oven! Inside a smokehouse, smoke surrounds the sheets of rubber, heating and drying them. In forest villages around the world, rubber is still created this way: rolled out by hand, and dried by sunshine or smoke. But today most rubber is produced in industrial laboratories and factories.

[5] **acid:** a very strong chemical

Often, as with tires and erasers, the use of rubber is obvious, but there are some uses of rubber that are more surprising. Some medical tools, for example, are dipped in latex. Natural latex is also important as an adhesive[6] in the production of envelopes, labels, sticky tape, and bandages. In fact, rubber is used in factories around the world as a raw material in all kinds of products, from airplanes to zippers.

Rubber – or the latex it is made from – may seem like a miracle product, but it can be dangerous. About 4 percent of Americans are allergic[7] to latex. People who are in contact with latex on a regular basis, such as hospital workers and industrial rubber workers, are two to three times more likely to suffer from latex allergies. Just touching a small amount, such as when putting on latex gloves, can cause the skin to become very irritated.

[6] **adhesive:** something that causes things to stick together, like glue
[7] **allergic:** can get sick from contact with

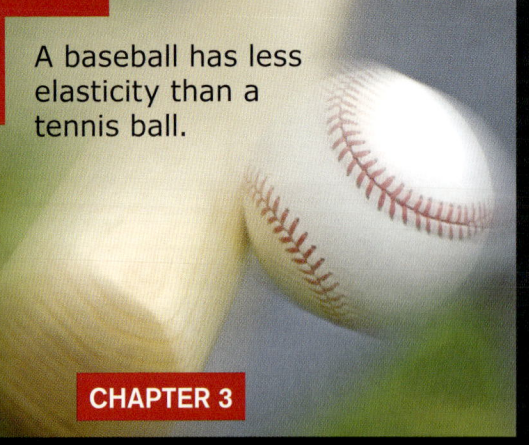

A baseball has less elasticity than a tennis ball.

CHAPTER 3

The Heart of Sports

EVERYONE LOVES FUN AND GAMES – AND RUBBER MAKES OUR GAMES A LOT MORE FUN!

    We put rubber in our sports shoes to get an extra bounce in our step. We need rubber for all the balls we love to hit and chase. We can have fun in water, too, thanks to rubber. No doubt about it, rubber is an ideal material for sporting equipment and clothing. You could even say that rubber is at the heart of modern sports!

    So what special quality does rubber have to make it especially useful in the sporting world? The magic word is *elasticity*!

    The special elasticity of natural rubber, and its potential for use in sports, was never a secret to people who lived near rubber trees! Solid rubber balls were used in games by the people of ancient Mesoamerica[8] as early as 1600 BCE. Rubber balls were so highly valued that they were also burned or buried in religious ceremonies.

[8] **Mesoamerica:** the area and early cultures of Central America

People played ball games in Europe, too, but until the first explorers saw the Mayans and the Aztecs playing with rubber balls, about 500 years ago, all European balls were made of wood and skins. When Spanish explorers saw the strange and surprising movement of bouncing rubber balls for the first time, they wrote in their diaries that the balls were bewitched![9]

Since then, however, people in Europe and elsewhere have been enjoying playing sports with balls made of this magical, **flexible** material. Golf balls, for example. Three hundred years ago, golf balls were made of wood, or tiny bags stuffed with goose feathers. Today, the heart of a golf ball is solid rubber. Other balls such as basketballs and soccer balls contain a rubber bladder – an airtight pocket – full of compressed air. The bladder is what gives a ball its lightness and bounce.

There are other ways that rubber's elasticity is used in sports and **recreation**. Huge elastic cords are used in bungee jumping. This activity began in the jungles of Vanuatu, an island nation in the South Pacific Ocean, where young men jumped off platforms with vines[10] tied to their feet to show courage. Today's bungee cords are made of hundreds of long pieces of rubber. Would you trust your life to the strength and elasticity of rubber?

[9]**bewitched:** controlled by magical or unnatural forces
[10]**vine:** a type of plant that grows in long, twisting pieces

Converse All-Stars aren't just for basketball.

The history of sports shoes also shows the importance of rubber. At the end of the 19th century, the US Rubber Company invented shoes that were made of a heavy cloth called canvas and had rubber soles. The new shoes were nicknamed *sneakers* because, thanks to their soft soles, a person wearing them could sneak up on[11] someone.

Sneakers soon became extremely popular. Athletes especially liked them because the rubber soles kept the shoes, and the athletes, from sliding on the floor during games. The shoes were firm but flexible and allowed athletes to change direction more quickly, which made the games more exciting to play and watch.

[11] **sneak up on:** approach quietly and unnoticed

In 1917, the Converse Rubber Shoe Company designed a basketball shoe, the Converse All-Star. Though redesigned over the years, these shoes are still popular today.

In 1924, German brothers Adi and Rudi Dassler, began making sports shoes. Adi convinced Jesse Owens, the American runner, to wear their special running shoes at the 1936 Berlin Olympics. Owens won four gold medals and the Dassler brothers won commercial success. Interestingly, the brothers later started their own separate companies. Adi Dassler started Adidas, and Rudi started Puma.

Today, Nike's Air Jordan is one of the world's most popular types of sports shoe, selling five million pairs annually. The simple sneaker has become a fashion necessity as well as a sporting one!

Air Jordans are very popular sport shoes.

Many sports stadiums use artificial turf instead of grass.

Because rubber is also an excellent insulating[12] material, it is used in wetsuits. Wetsuits are important in a variety of water sports, such as surfing, scuba diving, kayaking, and windsurfing. Wetsuits keep us warm because the material reduces the amount of body heat that can escape from inside the suit.

[12]**insulate:** use something to prevent heat, water, electricity, etc., from escaping or entering

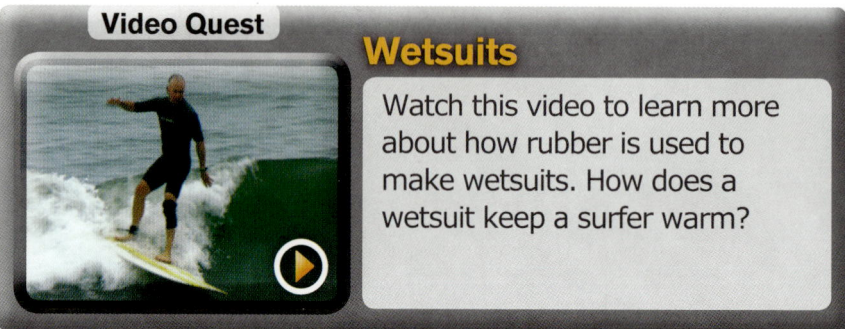

Video Quest

Wetsuits

Watch this video to learn more about how rubber is used to make wetsuits. How does a wetsuit keep a surfer warm?

16

? EVALUATE

What sports and recreation equipment do you use? How does rubber make the activities you do better or safer?

Rubber is also used as flooring for a great variety of sports. For example, sheets of rubber are placed under wooden dance floors, as a way to cushion the impact on the dancers' feet and legs. This is also the reason why gymnastics flooring is often made of rubber. Rubber is also used in the making and installation of artificial turf, which is commonly used in baseball, football, and soccer stadiums around the world instead of natural grass.

There's rubber on the floor, rubber in our shoes, and rubber in the sports equipment we use. Without rubber, the world of sports would be a very different place!

CHAPTER 4

Rolling Along

RUBBER HELPS KEEP US MOVING IN SPORTS, BUT IT ALSO KEEPS US MOVING ON THE ROAD, IN THE SKY – AND EVEN IN OUTER SPACE!

The history of modern methods of transport is closely linked with developments in rubber production. The first major development resulted from an accident.

In 1839, the American inventor Charles Goodyear was working with rubber in his lab and mistakenly dropped some sulfur[13] onto it. The resulting rubber was very strong, but still flexible. This was the beginning of vulcanization, a process that makes natural rubber even more useful.

Charles Goodyear invented vulcanization.

Another major development was the invention of the first pneumatic (air-filled) tire. In 1888, a Scottish veterinarian named John Dunlop noticed that his son got headaches from riding his tricycle, which had solid rubber tires. To improve things, this clever dad wrapped a tube around the wheel, then pumped air into it using a soccer ball pump! Dunlop went on to start the Dunlop Pneumatic Tyre Company.

[13]**sulfur (or sulphur):** a chemical with a strong smell, like bad eggs

Two years later, French brothers André and Edouard Michelin invented the first removable air-filled tire for bicycles. And in 1892 they thought of an interesting way to show off their new invention. They participated in a cycling race outside Paris. But first, they placed nails on the road, forcing people to see that changing tires was quick and easy!

These two important developments had a great impact on the automobile industry. The first automobiles, manufactured in the United States and Europe at the end of the 19th century, had tires made of solid rubber placed around wheels made of steel. It was probably not a very smooth ride!

In 1895, the Michelin brothers moved from bikes to cars and introduced the first pneumatic automobile tire. These tires provided a more comfortable ride while being as strong as solid rubber tires.

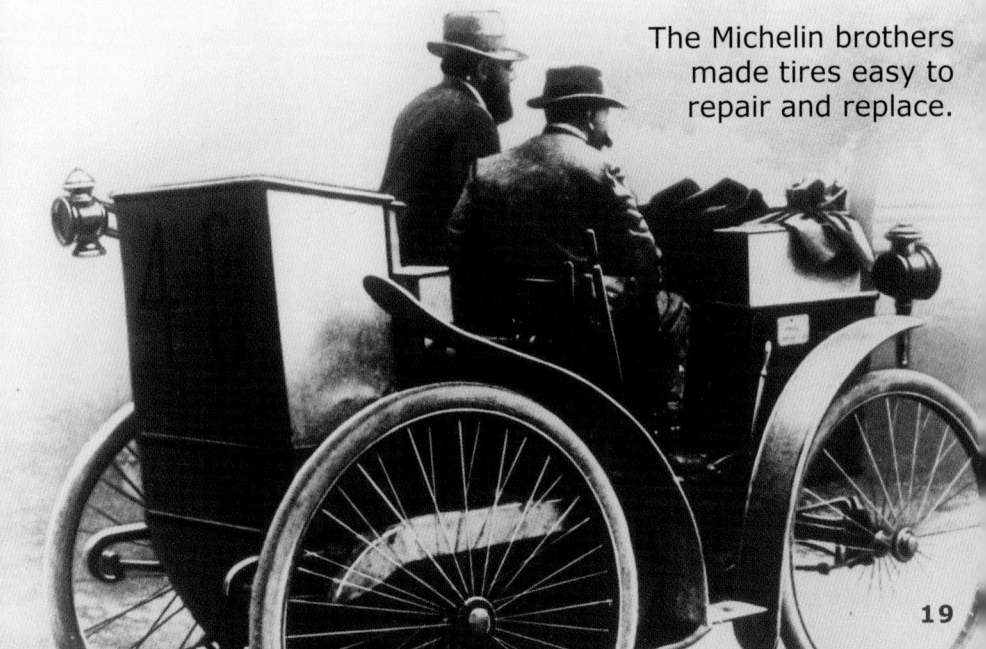

The Michelin brothers made tires easy to repair and replace.

The Michelin tire company eventually became hugely successful, but the first commercially successful automobile tire was American. It was invented by Philip Strauss in 1911 and marketed by his company, the Hardman Tire and Rubber Company. Strauss's original tire design included an inner-tube filled with air. It was soon preferred to solid rubber car tires, because the air-filled tires were thought to cause less damage to roads.

The success of Strauss's tires was made possible because of all the improvements to rubber tires that had been made during the previous decade. In 1908, Frank Seiberling thought of cutting lines, called treads, into tires as a way to prevent cars from slipping on wet roads. And in 1910, the Goodrich Company added the chemical carbon to the rubber, which made their tires last longer.

Modern society was closely connected to the automobile from that time onwards – and there was no turning back! Thanks to improvements in auto engines, and plenty of cheap gasoline, car-driving soon became more than a form of recreation for the rich. It was a growing necessity for all kinds of people.

As the demand for rubber increased, the cost of natural rubber increased, too. Scientists at rubber companies and other laboratories in the industrialized world started working hard to find a way to make inexpensive **synthetic** rubber.

Several types of synthetic rubber were invented during the 1930s, in Germany, Russia, and the United States. This was done by adding oil to the latex. In 1937, the B.F. Goodrich Company of Ohio, USA, produced the first tires made of synthetic rubber.

UNDERSTAND
Why was there an increase in the demand for natural rubber in the early 20th century?

Production of synthetic rubber didn't really take off, however, until World War II, when the US government demanded that industry develop an alternative to natural rubber. In 1940, Goodrich invented a cheap synthetic rubber called Ameripol. This product, which was stronger than natural rubber, soon became even cheaper to produce, and by 1944, natural rubber production was already only half that of synthetic rubber production.

The demand for rubber increased in the 1940s because of World War II.

During the economically productive years after World War II, demand for rubber continued to grow. Rubber is an important material in road construction, as an ingredient in asphalt. As road networks grew, so did our need for asphalt, and our dependence on rubber. Cars also became more affordable, so their use for business and pleasure grew enormously. Perhaps partly as a result of this, motorsports such as NASCAR and Formula One racing became popular.

Rubber is also necessary in the aviation[14] industry. Goodyear makes tires for airplanes, and Michelin supplies the tires for the Space Shuttle program. Rubber is also now being used as a raw material in the production of solid fuel for rockets and other types of spacecraft. Solid fuel is safer and more convenient to transport than liquid fuels, like gasoline.

Rubber is essential to modern life, but it is also a growing problem. We know how to make good use of rubber, but do we know what to do with it after we've finished with it?

It seems that scientists of the past might have done their job too well. Take tires, for example. The qualities that make them useful to us – strength and durability[15] – are the same qualities that make them difficult to get rid of! Up to now, we buried old tires or just threw them onto "tire mountains." But these methods carry the risk of fire and pollution. The challenge for the rubber industry today is how to destroy or recycle products responsibly, how to "unmake" the miracle of rubber.

[14]**aviation:** the science of flight
[15]**durability:** lasting a long time

Video Quest

Tire Mountains

Watch this video to learn about tire mountains. How long have these tires been stored at this landfill?

CHAPTER 5

What Do You Think?

**YOU BE THE INVENTOR –
OF NEW USES FOR OLD RUBBER!**

Rubber only used to be found in trees in the Amazon rainforest, but now it's everywhere. It's in the bathroom. It's in the kitchen. It's even in our refrigerators. It's in outer space, and on the soles of our shoes. We couldn't get rid of it if we tried.

In the early years, no one could imagine having too much of this great natural and man-made material that makes our lives so much easier. But now, many people are warning that too much rubber is exactly what we have, and we have to find ways to recycle it.

Here are some ways some people are using old tires:

- Gardening: Tires make excellent garden borders and containers for plants. The chemicals used in the rubber do not go into the ground, and water doesn't damage or destroy them.
- Play equipment: With just a long rope and a tall tree, you can turn an old tire into a swing.
- Building material: Fill tires with dirt and they make a strong, waterproof wall for any type of building. Just add a roof!

Can you think of other new ways to use old rubber?

After You Read

Do You Know?

Choose the correct answer.

1 The first European explorers saw native people using latex to make shoes, toys, tools, and for what other purpose?
- Ⓐ to make bandages
- Ⓑ to drink
- Ⓒ to make "Indian rubber"
- Ⓓ to light their homes

2 Henry Wickham secretly took seeds from Brazil to what other place?
- Ⓐ the Amazon River
- Ⓑ Asia
- Ⓒ Africa
- Ⓓ London

3 What is the purpose of tree sap?
- Ⓐ to give water to the tree
- Ⓑ to keep the leaves soft and wet
- Ⓒ to carry sugars and nutrients to parts of the tree
- Ⓓ to kill insects that try to eat the leaves

4 A rubber tree can produce about how many kilograms of latex in one year?
- Ⓐ 6
- Ⓑ 11
- Ⓒ 100
- Ⓓ 225

5 Why is rubber put under wooden dance floors?
- Ⓐ to cushion the impact on dancers' knees and feet
- Ⓑ to make dancers able to jump very high
- Ⓒ to protect the floor from the impact of the dancing
- Ⓓ to reduce the sound of the dancers' feet when they move

6 Which sports shoe sells about five million pairs every year?
- Ⓐ Converse All-Star
- Ⓑ Adidas sneakers
- Ⓒ Nike Air Jordan
- Ⓓ The Puma "Rudi"

7 What is a "tire mountain"?
- Ⓐ a work of art
- Ⓑ a tourist spot
- Ⓒ a place where races are held
- Ⓓ piles of old, used tires

Complete the Text

Complete this paragraph with the correct words from the box.

| asphalt | pneumatic | recycle | synthetic | vulcanization |

    Charles Goodyear accidentally found a way to make natural rubber stronger, a process called ❶ _____. Later, John Dunlop made the first ❷ _____ tire, for his son's tricycle. During World War II, a cheap ❸ _____ rubber called Ameripol was invented. After the War, rubber was used, not just to make shoes, toys, tires, and rocket fuel, but also ❹ _____, a material used for building roads. Now we have too much rubber in our world. We need to find ways to ❺ _____ the rubber we have thrown away.

Answer Key

Words to Know, page 4
1 Latex **2** tap **3** raw material **4** sole **5** Elasticity
6 synthetic

Words to Know, page 5
Recreation (in any order): wetsuit, bungee cords, artificial turf
Transport (in any order): tire, asphalt, treads

Apply, page 5
Answers will vary.

Video Quest, page 9
Rubber plantations were first developed in Brazil.

Video Quest, page 16
A wetsuit uses the person's own body heat to warm a thin layer of water inside the suit.

Evaluate, page 17
Answers will vary.

Understand, page 21
Improvements in automobiles and cheap gasoline made it possible for anyone to drive, not just rich people, so more cars and tires were needed.

Video Quest, page 23
These tires have been stored at this landfill for ten years.

Do You Know?, page 26
1 D **2** D **3** C **4** B **5** A **6** C **7** D

Complete the Text, page 27
1 vulcanization **2** pneumatic **3** synthetic **4** asphalt
5 recycle